SPACETOP

G1

A COMPREHENSIVE USER GUIDE TO MAXIMIZING YOUR WORKFLOW WITH THE WORLD'S FIRST SCREENLESS LAPTOP

HARPER PIPER

Copyright *HARPER PIPER, 2024.*

All rights reserved. No part of this publication may be reproduced, distributed, or transmitted in any form or by any means, including photocopying, recording, or other electronic or mechanical methods, without the prior written permission of the publisher, except in the case of brief quotations embodied in critical reviews and certain other non-commercial uses permitted by copyright law.

Table of Contents

Chapter 1 ___ 7
The Genesis of Spatial Computing ___ 7
Definition and Historical Background ___ 7
Key Milestones in AR and VR Development ___ 9

Chapter 2 ___ 13
The Rise of AR and VR in Consumer Technology ___ 13
Major Players and Innovations ___ 13
The Role of Spatial Computing in Modern Technology ___ 17

Chapter 3 ___ 21
Introducing Sightful and Its Vision ___ 21
Company Background and Mission ___ 21
Founders and Key Personnel ___ 22

Chapter 4 ___ 25
Conceptualizing the Spacetop G1 ___ 25
Initial Ideas and Inspirations ___ 25
Overcoming Design and Technological Challenges ___ 27

Chapter 5 ___ 31
Hardware Innovations ___ 31
Detailed Hardware Specifications ___ 31
Comparative Analysis with Traditional Laptops ___ 34

Chapter 6 — 39

The Power of AR Glasses — 39
- Design and Functionality of Xreal Glasses — 39
- User Experience and Comfort — 41

Chapter 7 — 45

Software and Operating System — 45
- Overview of SpaceOS — 45
- Integration of AI and AR in SpaceOS — 48

Chapter 8 — 51

Purchasing and Setup — 51
- How to Buy and Reserve a Spacetop G1 — 51
- Unboxing and Initial Setup — 53

Chapter 9 — 57

User Guide and Tips — 57
- Basic Navigation and Controls — 57
- Advanced Features and Customization — 59
- Work From Anywhere: Transforming Productivity — 62
- Entertainment and Beyond — 64
- Potential Uses in Gaming and Virtual Meetings — 65
- Troubleshooting the Spacetop G1: A Comprehensive Guide — 67
- General Troubleshooting Tips — 72

Chapter 1

The Genesis of Spatial Computing

Definition and Historical Background

Spatial computing represents a paradigm shift in how we interact with digital information, transcending traditional two-dimensional screens to create immersive, three-dimensional experiences that blend seamlessly with the physical world. At its core, spatial computing involves the use of augmented reality (AR), virtual reality (VR), and mixed reality (MR) technologies to manipulate and enhance real-world environments through digital overlays and virtual objects.

The concept of spatial computing can be traced back to the mid-20th century when early visionaries like Ivan Sutherland and Myron Krueger began exploring the potential of computer graphics and interactive environments. Sutherland's groundbreaking work in the 1960s, including the creation of the "Sketchpad" system and the invention of the first head-mounted display (HMD), laid the foundation for modern AR and VR technologies. His vision of a "Ultimate Display" foreshadowed a world where digital objects would be indistinguishable from physical ones, setting the stage for the future of spatial computing.

In the decades that followed, advancements in computer graphics, processing power, and sensor technologies propelled the field forward. The 1990s saw significant progress with the development of more sophisticated VR systems, such as the Virtuality arcade machines and the Sega VR headset. Despite their limitations, these early systems captured the imagination of both developers and users, sparking interest in immersive computing experiences.

Key Milestones in AR and VR Development

The journey of spatial computing is marked by several key milestones that have shaped its evolution and brought it closer to mainstream adoption.

1. The Advent of Augmented Reality:

- In 1992, Tom Caudell, a researcher at Boeing, coined the term "augmented reality" to describe a digital display used to guide workers in assembling aircraft. This early application demonstrated the practical potential of overlaying digital information onto the physical world.

2. The Arrival of Consumer VR:

- The mid-1990s witnessed the introduction of consumer-grade VR systems, such as the Virtual Boy by Nintendo and the VFX1 Headgear by Forte Technologies. While these products were commercial failures, they highlighted the growing interest in VR and the need for more advanced technology.

3. The Rise of Mobile AR:

- The 2000s brought significant advancements in mobile technology, leading to the development of AR applications for smartphones. In 2009, the

AR browser "Layar" allowed users to view contextual information overlaid on their camera feed, paving the way for popular AR apps like Pokémon Go in 2016.

4. Modern VR Renaissance:

- The launch of the Oculus Rift Kickstarter campaign in 2012 marked a turning point for VR. Developed by Palmer Luckey, the Oculus Rift headset garnered widespread attention and funding, ultimately leading to Facebook's acquisition of Oculus VR in 2014. This event revitalized interest in VR and spurred the development of competing headsets like the HTC Vive and PlayStation VR.

5. AR and MR in the Enterprise:

- Microsoft's introduction of the HoloLens in 2015 brought mixed reality to the forefront. The HoloLens combined AR with spatial mapping, allowing users to interact with digital objects as if they were part of the physical environment. This innovation found applications in various industries, from healthcare to engineering, showcasing the practical benefits of spatial computing.

6. The Advent of Lightweight AR Glasses:

- Recent advancements have focused on creating more compact and comfortable AR devices. Companies like Google, with its Google Glass, and Magic Leap, with the Magic Leap One, have made strides in developing lightweight AR glasses that integrate seamlessly into daily life. These devices aim to provide users with persistent, context-aware digital information without the bulkiness of traditional headsets.

7. Spatial Computing in Everyday Life:

- The integration of AR and VR into consumer products, such as smartphones and gaming consoles, has made spatial computing more accessible. Apple's ARKit and Google's ARCore have empowered developers to create a wide range of AR applications, from interactive games to educational tools, making spatial computing a part of everyday life.

Chapter 2

The Rise of AR and VR in Consumer Technology

Major Players and Innovations

The evolution of augmented reality (AR) and virtual reality (VR) technologies has seen the rise of several key players and groundbreaking innovations that have significantly shaped the landscape of consumer technology.

1. Oculus VR and the Rift:

- ***Palmer Luckey*** revolutionized the VR industry with the introduction of the Oculus Rift in 2012. The Kickstarter campaign for the Oculus Rift garnered unprecedented support, signaling strong consumer interest in VR. Facebook's acquisition of Oculus VR in 2014 for $2 billion underscored the potential of VR technology, leading to further advancements and the eventual release of the Oculus Rift in 2016.

2. HTC and the Vive:

- ***HTC,*** in collaboration with Valve Corporation, launched the HTC Vive in 2016. The Vive distinguished itself with room-scale VR, allowing users to move freely within a physical space while interacting with a virtual environment. This innovation set a new standard for immersive VR experiences and highlighted the importance of spatial tracking.

3. Sony and PlayStation VR:

- ***Sony*** entered the VR market with the PlayStation VR (PSVR) in 2016, leveraging its PlayStation console ecosystem to offer an accessible VR experience to millions of gamers. The PSVR's integration with the PlayStation 4 provided a high-quality, console-based VR experience at a relatively affordable price point, making VR more mainstream.

4. Google and ARCore:

- ***Google*** has been a significant player in the AR space, starting with Google Glass in 2013, which brought AR to a wearable form factor. Despite its limited commercial success, Google Glass laid the groundwork for future AR developments.

Google's ARCore, introduced in 2017, enabled developers to create AR applications for millions of Android devices, democratizing AR technology and fostering a vibrant ecosystem of AR apps.

5. Apple and ARKit:

- ***Apple*** launched ARKit in 2017, providing developers with a robust framework to build AR applications for iOS devices. With its focus on seamless integration with the iPhone and iPad's hardware, ARKit allowed users to experience high-quality AR without additional equipment. Apple's continued investment in AR, as evidenced by its later announcements like the Vision Pro headset, reflects its commitment to leading in the spatial computing space.

6. Microsoft and HoloLens:

- ***Microsoft*** made a significant impact with the HoloLens, an AR headset introduced in 2015 that combined augmented and mixed reality. The HoloLens featured advanced spatial mapping and interaction capabilities, making it ideal for enterprise applications in fields like healthcare, engineering, and design. Microsoft's push for mixed reality emphasized the practical applications of AR in professional settings.

7. Magic Leap:

- *Magic Leap,* founded in 2010, gained attention for its ambitious vision of AR with the release of the Magic Leap One in 2018. The device featured advanced optics and spatial computing capabilities, aiming to create a seamless blend of digital and physical worlds. Although it faced challenges in gaining widespread consumer adoption, Magic Leap's innovations influenced the development of AR technology.

8. Niantic and Pokémon Go:

- *Niantic* brought AR to the masses with the release of Pokémon Go in 2016. This mobile game used AR to overlay virtual Pokémon onto real-world locations, creating an engaging and immersive gaming experience. Pokémon Go's success demonstrated the potential of AR in entertainment and highlighted its ability to drive massive consumer engagement.

The Role of Spatial Computing in Modern Technology

Spatial computing has become a cornerstone of modern technology, transforming how we interact with digital information and our physical environments. By integrating digital elements into the real world, spatial computing enables more intuitive and immersive interactions, enhancing both consumer and professional experiences.

1. Enhanced Productivity and Collaboration:

   - Spatial computing has revolutionized remote work and collaboration. Tools like Microsoft HoloLens and various AR conferencing applications allow teams to interact with 3D models and shared virtual spaces, improving communication and productivity. These technologies enable professionals to visualize complex data, conduct virtual meetings, and collaborate on projects in real-time, regardless of physical location.

2. Education and Training:

   - In education, spatial computing provides immersive learning experiences that enhance understanding and retention. Students can explore historical sites in VR, interact with 3D anatomical models, and participate in virtual labs. In professional training, AR and VR simulations offer realistic practice environments for fields such as medicine, aviation, and manufacturing, reducing the risk and cost associated with traditional training methods.

3. Healthcare and Medicine:

- Spatial computing has transformative applications in healthcare. Surgeons can use AR to overlay critical information onto a patient's body during operations, improving precision and outcomes. VR therapy is used to treat conditions like PTSD and phobias by providing controlled, immersive environments for exposure therapy. Additionally, AR-assisted diagnosis and remote consultations expand access to medical expertise.

4. Retail and E-commerce:

- AR enhances the retail experience by allowing customers to visualize products in their real environment before purchasing. Companies like IKEA and Amazon offer AR apps that let users see how furniture or decor will look in their homes. This reduces return rates and increases customer satisfaction by ensuring better-informed purchasing decisions.

5. Entertainment and Gaming:

- Spatial computing has expanded the possibilities in entertainment and gaming. VR games provide deeply immersive experiences that transport players to entirely new worlds. AR gaming, exemplified by Pokémon Go, blends the digital and physical worlds, encouraging real-world exploration and social interaction. Additionally, immersive storytelling in VR offers new ways for audiences to experience narratives.

6. Architecture and Real Estate:

- Architects and real estate professionals use spatial computing to create virtual walkthroughs of buildings and properties. Clients can explore detailed 3D models, making it easier to understand design concepts and make informed decisions. This technology accelerates the design process, improves client satisfaction, and reduces the need for physical prototypes.

7. Automotive Industry:

- The automotive industry leverages AR for design, manufacturing, and customer experience.

AR displays in vehicles provide real-time information on navigation, safety, and vehicle performance, enhancing driver awareness. In design and manufacturing, VR simulations streamline the development process, allowing engineers to test and refine designs in a virtual environment.

Chapter 3

Introducing Sightful and Its Vision

Company Background and Mission

The genesis of Sightful is rooted in a profound belief in the potential of AR technology to transform productivity and connectivity. The company envisions a world where physical screens are obsolete, replaced by virtual workspaces that can be accessed anytime, anywhere. Sightful's flagship product, the Spacetop G1, epitomizes this vision. It is a screenless laptop that, when paired with AR glasses, creates a 100-inch virtual workspace, offering users a vast, customizable digital environment without the need for a physical screen.

Sightful's approach to spatial computing is grounded in practical applications that enhance daily life. By focusing on productivity rather than entertainment, the company differentiates itself from other tech giants in the AR space. Sightful's products are designed to meet the needs of remote workers, digital nomads, and anyone seeking a more flexible and immersive computing experience.

Founders and Key Personnel

Sightful was founded by **Tamir Berliner** and **Tom Rabinovich,** two visionaries with extensive experience in the AR and tech industries. Their combined expertise and passion for innovation have been instrumental in shaping Sightful's unique approach to spatial computing.

Tamir Berliner, the CEO of Sightful, has a rich background in augmented reality, having previously worked at Magic Leap, a pioneer in the AR field. During his time at Magic Leap, Berliner gained invaluable insights into the challenges and opportunities within the AR industry. His experience there fueled his desire to create a product that addressed the limitations of existing AR devices, particularly the bulkiness and discomfort of headsets. Berliner's vision for Sightful is driven by a commitment to enhancing user comfort and productivity through cutting-edge technology.

Tom Rabinovich, the CTO of Sightful, brings a wealth of technical expertise to the company. With a background in software development and engineering, Rabinovich has been instrumental in developing the proprietary operating system, SpaceOS, that powers the Spacetop G1. His technical acumen ensures that Sightful's products are not only innovative but also reliable and user-friendly. Rabinovich's role is crucial in transforming the company's vision into tangible, high-performance products.

The core team at Sightful is composed of experts in various fields, including software development, hardware engineering, and user experience design. This multidisciplinary team collaborates closely to ensure that every aspect of Sightful's products meets the highest standards of quality and functionality. The team's collective expertise enables Sightful to push the boundaries of what is possible in spatial computing, continually refining and improving their products based on user feedback and technological advancements.

Chapter 4

Conceptualizing the Spacetop G1

Initial Ideas and Inspirations

The genesis of the Spacetop G1 began with a simple yet revolutionary idea: to liberate users from the constraints of physical screens. This concept was born from the collective experiences of Sightful's founders, Tamir Berliner and Tom Rabinovich, who had both spent years immersed in the world of augmented reality (AR) and spatial computing. Their work at companies like Magic Leap exposed them to the immense potential of AR, but also to its significant limitations—bulky headsets, limited battery life, and a user experience that often felt more like a novelty than a practical tool.

Berliner and Rabinovich envisioned a future where AR could be seamlessly integrated into daily life, enhancing productivity and connectivity without the cumbersome hardware. They imagined a world where a vast, immersive digital workspace could be accessed anywhere, anytime, simply by putting on a pair of AR glasses. This vision was the spark that ignited the creation of the Spacetop G1, the world's first screenless laptop.

The inspiration for the Spacetop G1 also came from observing the evolving needs of modern workers. The rise of remote work and digital nomadism highlighted the limitations of traditional laptops. People needed more flexibility and the ability to work from anywhere without sacrificing productivity. Berliner and Rabinovich saw an opportunity to create a device that would meet these needs by leveraging AR technology to provide an expansive, customizable workspace that could be carried in a backpack.

Overcoming Design and Technological Challenges

Turning this visionary idea into a reality, however, was no small feat. The development of the Spacetop G1 involved overcoming numerous design and technological challenges. One of the most significant hurdles was creating a device that was both powerful and portable. The team needed to pack the capabilities of a high-performance laptop into a compact, screenless form factor, all while ensuring a seamless and intuitive user experience.

1. Miniaturization and Hardware Integration:

- The first challenge was miniaturizing the necessary hardware without compromising performance. This required innovative engineering solutions and close collaboration with partners like Qualcomm and XREAL. The Qualcomm Snapdragon QCS8550 processor was chosen for its powerful yet efficient performance, enabling the Spacetop G1 to handle demanding applications while maintaining a sleek and lightweight design. Integrating the AR glasses, developed in partnership with XREAL, posed its own set of challenges. The glasses needed to be lightweight, comfortable for extended wear, and capable of delivering high-quality visuals. The result was a pair of glasses featuring advanced OLED screens, open-ear speakers, and ergonomic design, providing a seamless user experience.

2. Developing SpaceOS:

- Another major challenge was developing the proprietary operating system, SpaceOS. Unlike traditional operating systems, SpaceOS needed to function intuitively in a 3D space, allowing users to interact with multiple virtual windows and applications in an immersive environment. Rabinovich led the software development team in creating a user-friendly interface that leveraged AR's potential while remaining accessible to those accustomed to 2D screens. The operating system had to be robust and versatile, capable of running web applications, managing multitasking efficiently, and providing a stable platform for future updates and enhancements.

3. User Experience and Ergonomics:

- Ensuring a positive user experience was paramount. The design team had to consider ergonomics carefully, given that users would be wearing AR glasses for extended periods. The glasses were designed to be lightweight and adjustable, with automatic dimming features to adapt to different lighting conditions. Additionally, the Spacetop G1's physical design needed to be intuitive, with a familiar keyboard and trackpad setup that minimized the learning curve for new users.

4. Battery Life and Portability:

   - Battery life was another critical factor. Users needed a device that could last through a typical workday. The team optimized the Spacetop G1's power consumption, enabling up to eight hours of battery life on a single charge. Achieving this balance between performance and battery efficiency was essential for making the device practical for everyday use.

5. Real-World Testing and Feedback:

   - Throughout the development process, real-world testing and user feedback were crucial. Sightful launched an invite-only early access program to gather insights from a diverse group of users. This feedback was instrumental in refining both the hardware and software. Adjustments were made based on user experiences, leading to improvements in processing power, comfort, and overall usability.

Chapter 5

Hardware Innovations

Detailed Hardware Specifications

The Spacetop G1 represents a leap forward in the integration of augmented reality (AR) and computing technology. Its hardware is designed to provide a seamless, high-performance experience while maintaining a sleek and portable form factor. Here's a detailed look at the key hardware specifications that make the Spacetop G1 stand out:

- **Processor:** Qualcomm Snapdragon QCS8550

  - This powerful system-on-chip (SoC) is built to handle the demanding requirements of AR applications while maintaining energy efficiency. The Snapdragon QCS8550 delivers high processing power and is optimized for multitasking and AI computations.

- **Graphics:** Adreno 740 GPU

  - The Adreno 740 GPU ensures smooth and responsive graphics, capable of rendering high-resolution content for the AR glasses. It supports a 90Hz refresh rate, providing fluid visual experiences essential for immersive AR environments.

- **Memory:** 16GB LPDDR5 RAM

  - This substantial memory capacity allows for efficient multitasking, ensuring that users can run multiple applications simultaneously without experiencing lag.

- **Storage:** 128GB UFS 3.1

  - The 128GB of Universal Flash Storage (UFS) 3.1 offers fast read and write speeds, reducing load times for applications and enhancing overall system performance.

- **Display:** AR Glasses by XREAL

  - The AR glasses feature dual OLED displays, each with a resolution of 1920 x 1080 pixels. They provide a virtual screen equivalent to 100 inches, with a 50-degree field of view and 42 pixels per degree. The glasses are designed for comfort and long-term wear, with built-in speakers and automatic dimming to adapt to various lighting conditions.

- Connectivity: Wi-Fi 7, Bluetooth 5.3, 5G

- Advanced connectivity options ensure that the Spacetop G1 can maintain fast and stable connections, whether for downloading large files, streaming content, or connecting peripherals.

- Battery Life: Up to 8 hours

- The Spacetop G1 is designed to last a full workday on a single charge, making it a practical choice for remote work and travel.

- Ports: 2x USB-C

- The inclusion of USB-C ports provides flexibility for charging, data transfer, and connecting external devices.

- Dimensions: 11.81 x 9.09 x 0.51-2.44 inches

- The compact size of the Spacetop G1 makes it highly portable, fitting easily into a backpack or laptop sleeve.

- **Weight:** 3.08 lbs (laptop), 0.18 lbs (glasses)

- The lightweight design of both the laptop and glasses enhances portability and comfort during extended use.

- **Webcam:** 5MP

- The integrated webcam is discreetly housed within the folding cover, ready for use during video calls and virtual meetings.

Comparative Analysis with Traditional Laptops

To understand the significance of the Spacetop G1's innovations, it's essential to compare it with traditional laptops across several key dimensions:

1. Display:

- *Traditional Laptops:* Typically feature built-in screens ranging from 13 to 17 inches. These screens are fixed in size and offer limited flexibility in terms of viewing angles and placement.

- *Spacetop G1:* Offers a virtual screen equivalent to 100 inches through AR glasses. This allows users to customize their workspace by positioning multiple virtual windows around them, creating an immersive and expansive digital environment.

2. Portability:

- ***Traditional Laptops:*** Often vary in weight, with ultra-portable models weighing around 2 to 3 pounds and gaming or high-performance laptops weighing upwards of 4 pounds.

- ***Spacetop G1:*** Combines a lightweight laptop base with ultra-light AR glasses. The total weight is comparable to that of a traditional laptop, but the lack of a physical screen and the compact design enhance its portability.

3. User Experience:

- ***Traditional Laptops:*** Users are confined to the fixed size and position of the laptop screen, often requiring additional monitors for expanded workspace.

- ***Spacetop G1:*** The AR glasses provide a dynamic and flexible workspace. Users can place virtual windows in their field of view, reducing the need to look down at a fixed screen and potentially improving ergonomics and productivity.

4. Battery Life:

- ***Traditional Laptops:*** Battery life varies widely, typically ranging from 6 to 12 hours depending on usage and the laptop's power profile.

- ***Spacetop G1:*** Offers up to 8 hours of battery life, aligning with the demands of a typical workday while balancing the power needs of its advanced AR features.

5. Performance:

- ***Traditional Laptops:*** Often feature a wide range of processors from Intel and AMD, with performance varying based on the intended use (e.g., general computing, gaming, professional applications).

- ***Spacetop G1:*** Utilizes the Qualcomm Snapdragon QCS8550, which, while not as powerful as high-end laptop CPUs, is optimized for AR applications and energy efficiency. It provides sufficient performance for productivity tasks, web applications, and multimedia consumption.

6. Innovative Features:

- ***Traditional Laptops:*** Include a range of features such as high-resolution displays, touchscreens, 2-in-1 convertibility, and high-performance GPUs for gaming and professional workstations.

- ***Spacetop G1:*** Introduces groundbreaking AR integration with a spatial operating system (SpaceOS), tailored for a 3D interactive experience. The glasses incorporate OLED technology for clear and vibrant visuals, with a design optimized for long-term comfort.

Chapter 6

The Power of AR Glasses

Design and Functionality of Xreal Glasses

The AR glasses included with the Spacetop G1 are designed by Xreal, a leading developer of augmented reality solutions. These glasses are a critical component of the Spacetop G1, transforming the traditional laptop experience into an immersive, spatial computing environment. Here's a detailed look at their design and functionality:

Design:

- ***Lightweight and Stylish:*** The Xreal glasses weigh just 0.18 lbs, making them one of the lightest AR glasses available. Their sleek design ensures they are not only functional but also fashionable, appealing to both tech enthusiasts and professionals.

- ***Dual OLED Displays:*** Each lens features an OLED display with a resolution of 1920 x 1080 pixels, providing sharp and vibrant visuals. This technology ensures high color accuracy and deep contrasts, enhancing the overall visual experience.

- **Wide Field of View:** The glasses offer a 50-degree diagonal field of view, which, combined with the high resolution, creates an expansive and immersive visual environment. This wide field of view is crucial for effectively simulating a large virtual workspace.

- **Adjustable Fit:** The glasses are designed to be adjustable, accommodating a wide range of head sizes and shapes. This ensures a comfortable fit for prolonged use.

Functionality:

- **Integrated Speakers:** Built-in open-ear speakers provide high-quality audio without the need for additional headphones. This allows users to stay aware of their surroundings while immersed in their virtual workspace.

- **Six Degrees of Freedom (6DoF):** The glasses track head movements in six degrees of freedom, allowing for precise control and interaction with virtual objects. This is essential for creating a seamless AR experience where users can move naturally and interact with digital content as if it were part of the real world.

- **_Connectivity:_** The glasses are hardwired to the Spacetop G1, ensuring a stable and low-latency connection. This direct connection is vital for maintaining high performance and responsiveness during use.

- **_Automatic Dimming:_** The glasses can automatically adjust their brightness based on ambient light conditions. This feature helps maintain visual clarity and reduces eye strain, especially in varying lighting environments.

User Experience and Comfort

The design and functionality of the Xreal glasses are meticulously crafted to provide an exceptional user experience, prioritizing both comfort and usability. Here's how these elements contribute to the overall user experience:

Comfort:

- **_Long-term Wearability:_** The lightweight design ensures that the glasses can be worn comfortably for extended periods. This is particularly important for users who need to work long hours without experiencing discomfort or fatigue.

- **Ergonomic Fit:** The adjustable fit and lightweight materials reduce pressure points on the nose and ears, enhancing overall comfort. Users can adjust the glasses to fit snugly without causing strain.

- **Prescription Inserts:** For users who wear prescription glasses, Xreal offers custom prescription inserts. This eliminates the need to wear the AR glasses over regular glasses, which can be cumbersome and uncomfortable.

User Experience:

- **Immersive Visuals:** The dual OLED displays provide a crisp, high-definition visual experience. The high pixel density and wide field of view create an immersive virtual workspace, making digital content appear as if it is floating in the real world.

- **Seamless Integration:** The glasses work seamlessly with the Spacetop G1, allowing users to interact with their digital environment effortlessly. The 6DoF tracking ensures that virtual objects stay anchored in place, even as the user moves their head or changes position.

- ***Multi-Tasking Capabilities:*** Users can open multiple virtual windows and place them around their field of view. This spatial arrangement of applications allows for efficient multitasking, as users can organize their workspace in a way that best suits their workflow.

- ***Ambient Awareness:*** The open-ear speaker design ensures that users remain aware of their surroundings while using the glasses. This is particularly useful in environments where situational awareness is important, such as offices or public spaces.

Chapter 7

Software and Operating System

Overview of SpaceOS

SpaceOS, the proprietary operating system developed by Sightful, is the heart of the Spacetop G1's groundbreaking technology. Built on an Android framework, SpaceOS is specifically designed to leverage the capabilities of augmented reality (AR), transforming the traditional laptop experience into a dynamic, spatial computing environment.

User Interface and Experience:

- *Intuitive Design:* SpaceOS features an intuitive user interface that seamlessly integrates with the AR capabilities of the Spacetop G1. Users navigate through a virtual workspace where applications and tools are spatially arranged, rather than confined to a flat screen.

- *Customizable Workspace:* Users can open multiple virtual windows and place them around their field of view, organizing their workspace in three dimensions. This spatial arrangement facilitates efficient multitasking and enhances productivity, as users can quickly access and manage various applications without the clutter of overlapping windows.

- **Gestural Controls:** SpaceOS supports a range of gestural controls, allowing users to interact with their virtual environment naturally. Simple gestures can be used to open, move, resize, and close applications, providing a hands-free and immersive experience.

- **Voice Commands:** Integrated voice recognition technology enables users to control SpaceOS using voice commands, adding another layer of convenience and accessibility.

Application Compatibility:

- **Web Applications:** At launch, SpaceOS supports a variety of web applications, enabling users to perform essential tasks such as browsing the internet, checking email, and participating in video conferences. Applications like Google Workspace, Microsoft 365, Slack, and Zoom are fully compatible, ensuring users have access to the tools they need.

- Android Apps: While initial support focuses on web applications, Sightful plans to expand SpaceOS to include dedicated Android apps. This future integration will provide users with access to a broader range of applications and services, enhancing the functionality of the Spacetop G1.

- Productivity Tools: SpaceOS includes built-in productivity tools tailored for AR use, such as virtual whiteboards, collaborative workspaces, and enhanced file management systems. These tools are designed to maximize the benefits of spatial computing in professional environments.

Integration of AI and AR in SpaceOS

The integration of artificial intelligence (AI) and augmented reality (AR) in SpaceOS is what truly sets it apart from other operating systems, creating a sophisticated and adaptive environment that enhances user productivity and engagement.

AI-Driven Features:

- ***Personalized Assistance:*** SpaceOS incorporates AI-driven personal assistants that can learn from user behavior and preferences. These assistants provide contextual recommendations, automate routine tasks, and offer real-time support, making the overall experience more efficient and user-friendly.

- ***Smart Notifications:*** The AI engine in SpaceOS intelligently prioritizes and manages notifications, ensuring that users are alerted to important updates without being overwhelmed by distractions. Notifications can be customized based on user preferences and work habits.

- ***Contextual Awareness:*** AI enhances the contextual awareness of the operating system, allowing it to understand the user's current activity and environment. This enables SpaceOS to provide relevant information and tools proactively, such as suggesting related documents during a meeting or adjusting settings based on ambient light.

Augmented Reality Enhancements:

- ***Virtual Displays:*** The core of SpaceOS's AR functionality lies in its ability to create and manage virtual displays. These displays can be positioned around the user's field of view, providing an expansive and immersive workspace that mimics multiple large monitors.

- ***Spatial Anchoring:*** Using AR technology, SpaceOS anchors virtual objects and applications to specific locations within the user's environment. This spatial anchoring ensures that virtual windows and tools remain in place, even as the user moves around, creating a stable and reliable workspace.

- ***Interactive 3D Models:*** For industries that rely on 3D modeling, such as architecture, engineering, and design, SpaceOS supports interactive 3D models that users can manipulate in real time. This capability allows for detailed inspections and collaborative discussions in a virtual space.

- ***Collaborative AR:*** SpaceOS facilitates collaborative AR experiences, enabling multiple users to interact with shared virtual objects and spaces. This feature is particularly beneficial for remote teams, allowing them to collaborate as if they were in the same physical location.

Performance Optimization:

- ***Efficient Resource Management:*** The integration of AI in SpaceOS also extends to resource management, optimizing the allocation of processing power and memory to ensure smooth performance. This is crucial for maintaining a high-quality AR experience without lag or interruptions.

- ***Adaptive Display Settings:*** SpaceOS can automatically adjust display settings based on user activity and environmental factors. For instance, the system can dim the AR glasses in bright environments to improve visibility or enhance contrast when viewing detailed information.

Chapter 8

Purchasing and Setup

How to Buy and Reserve a Spacetop G1

Purchasing a Spacetop G1 is a straightforward process, with Sightful offering a convenient online reservation system for interested buyers. Here's a step-by-step guide on how to buy and reserve a Spacetop G1:

1. Visit the Sightful Website: Navigate to the official Sightful website using a web browser on your computer or mobile device.

2. Product Page: Locate the product page for the Spacetop G1. This page will provide detailed information about the device, including specifications, pricing, and availability.

3. Reservation Option: Look for the option to reserve a Spacetop G1. This may be prominently displayed on the product page or accessible through a dedicated reservation portal.

4. Reservation Process: Follow the prompts to reserve your Spacetop G1. You may be required to provide some basic information, such as your name, email address, and shipping details.

5. Payment: Depending on the reservation system, you may be asked to make a reservation fee or deposit to secure your order. This fee is typically deducted from the total purchase price of the device.

6. Confirmation: Once your reservation is complete, you should receive a confirmation email or notification from Sightful. This will include details about your reservation and any next steps.

7. Finalize Purchase: After reserving your Spacetop G1, you may need to finalize the purchase when the device becomes available for shipment. This typically involves completing the payment process and providing any additional information required for shipping.

8. Shipping and Delivery: Once your Spacetop G1 is ready to ship, Sightful will arrange for delivery to your specified address. You should receive tracking information so you can monitor the progress of your shipment.

Unboxing and Initial Setup

When your Spacetop G1 arrives, you'll want to ensure a smooth and hassle-free setup process. Here's what to expect during unboxing and the initial setup:

1. Unboxing: Carefully unpack the Spacetop G1 from its shipping box. Inside, you'll find the Spacetop G1 laptop, along with any included accessories such as the AR glasses, charging cable, and documentation.

2. Inspect Contents: Take a moment to inspect the contents of the box for any signs of damage or missing items. If everything looks intact, proceed with the setup process.

3. Charging: Before powering on the Spacetop G1, ensure that it is adequately charged. Connect the charging cable to the laptop and plug it into a power source. Allow the device to charge until the battery indicator shows a sufficient charge level.

4. Power On: Once the Spacetop G1 is charged, press the power button to turn it on. Follow any on-screen prompts to begin the initial setup process.

5. Language and Region: Select your preferred language and region settings for the Spacetop G1. This will customize the device to your specific preferences and location.

6. Network Setup: Connect the Spacetop G1 to a Wi-Fi network to enable internet access. You may need to enter the network name and password to complete this step.

7. Software Updates: Check for any software updates available for the Spacetop G1. It's essential to keep the device's operating system and applications up to date to ensure optimal performance and security.

8. Account Setup: If prompted, sign in with your existing accounts or create new ones to access the Spacetop G1's features and services. This may include signing in with your Google or Microsoft account for email, cloud storage, and other services.

9. AR Glasses Setup: Follow the instructions to set up and pair the AR glasses with the Spacetop G1. This typically involves connecting the glasses to the laptop via a cable and adjusting the fit for comfort.

10. Tutorial and Tips: Take advantage of any tutorials or tips provided by Sightful to familiarize yourself with the Spacetop G1's features and capabilities. This will help you make the most of your new device from the start.

Once the initial setup is complete, you're ready to start using your Spacetop G1 and explore the possibilities of spatial computing in your daily workflow. Enjoy the seamless integration of AR technology and productivity tools as you embark on a new era of computing innovation.

Chapter 9

User Guide and Tips

Basic Navigation and Controls

Navigating and controlling the Spacetop G1 is intuitive and user-friendly, thanks to its innovative spatial computing interface. Here's a guide to basic navigation and controls:

1. Gestural Controls:

- ***Swipe:*** Use swiping gestures to navigate through virtual windows and applications. Swipe left or right to switch between open windows, and swipe up or down to scroll within applications.

- ***Pinch and Expand:*** Pinch inward or expand outward with two fingers to resize virtual windows. This allows you to adjust the size of windows to fit your preferences and workspace.

2. Voice Commands:

- ***Activate Assistant:*** Initiate the voice assistant by saying the wake word, such as "Hey, Spacetop." Once activated, you can issue commands or ask questions to perform various tasks.

- ***Commands:*** Use voice commands to open applications, search the web, set reminders, and more. The voice assistant responds to natural language inputs, making it easy to interact with the Spacetop G1 hands-free.

3. Physical Controls:

- ***Power Button:*** Press the power button to turn the Spacetop G1 on or off. This button is typically located on the side or front of the device.

- ***Volume Controls:*** Adjust the volume using dedicated volume buttons or controls on the Spacetop G1. These buttons allow you to increase or decrease the volume of audio output.

Advanced Features and Customization

Unlock the full potential of the Spacetop G1 with advanced features and customization options tailored to your preferences:

1. Multitasking and Productivity:

- ***Multi-Window Support:*** Take advantage of multi-window support to multitask efficiently. Open multiple virtual windows simultaneously and arrange them around your field of view for seamless productivity.

- ***Custom Layouts:*** Customize the layout of your virtual workspace to suit your workflow. Experiment with different arrangements of windows and applications to find the configuration that works best for you.

2. AR Integration:

- ***Interactive 3D Models:*** Explore interactive 3D models and visualizations in AR. Use gestures to manipulate and interact with virtual objects, gaining new insights and perspectives in various industries such as architecture, engineering, and design.

- ***Spatial Anchoring:*** Anchor virtual objects and applications to specific locations in your environment. This ensures that virtual content remains stable and aligned with the real world, enhancing immersion and usability.

3. Personalization:

- ***Theme and Wallpaper:*** Customize the theme and wallpaper of your virtual workspace to reflect your personal style. Choose from a range of themes and backgrounds to create a personalized and visually appealing environment.

- ***Voice Assistant Settings:*** Tailor the behavior and preferences of the voice assistant to meet your needs. Adjust settings such as language, voice recognition sensitivity, and response time to optimize the voice assistant experience.

4. Accessibility Features:

- ***Accessibility Settings:*** Explore accessibility settings to enhance usability for users with diverse needs. Adjust settings such as text size, color contrast, and audio feedback to improve accessibility and inclusivity.

5. Firmware Updates:

- ***Stay Up to Date:*** Keep your Spacetop G1 updated with the latest firmware and software updates. Regular updates provide new features, performance improvements, and security enhancements, ensuring that your device remains optimized and secure over time.

By familiarizing yourself with basic navigation and controls and exploring advanced features and customization options, you can maximize your productivity and enjoyment with the Spacetop G1. Experiment with different settings and configurations to tailor the device to your unique preferences and workflow, unlocking new possibilities in spatial computing.

Work From Anywhere: Transforming Productivity

The concept of "Work From Anywhere" (WFA) has gained significant traction in recent years, fueled by advancements in technology and changing work dynamics. The Spacetop G1 represents a groundbreaking innovation in the WFA landscape, offering users the freedom to work and collaborate from any location with unparalleled flexibility and efficiency.

Numerous case studies and user experiences highlight the transformative impact of the Spacetop G1 on productivity and collaboration in various industries and settings:

1. Remote Teams Collaboration:

- ***Case Study:*** A distributed team of software developers leverages the Spacetop G1 to collaborate on coding projects in real time. With virtual windows for code editors, communication tools, and project management software, team members can seamlessly coordinate their efforts and iterate on code, regardless of their physical location.

2. Architectural Design and Visualization:

- *User Experience:* An architectural firm adopts the Spacetop G1 for design reviews and client presentations. By showcasing interactive 3D models and virtual walkthroughs in AR, architects can engage clients in immersive design experiences, soliciting feedback and making design decisions more efficiently.

3. Remote Learning and Education:

- Case Study: A university integrates the Spacetop G1 into its remote learning initiatives, providing students with access to virtual classrooms and interactive educational content. Students can attend lectures, participate in discussions, and collaborate on projects using AR-enhanced learning materials, fostering a more engaging and immersive learning experience.

Entertainment and Beyond

The Spacetop G1 transcends traditional computing boundaries, offering a rich array of multimedia capabilities and unlocking new potential in entertainment, gaming, and virtual meetings.

Multimedia Capabilities

1. Streaming and Content Consumption:

- With its immersive AR interface, the Spacetop G1 provides an unparalleled platform for streaming movies, TV shows, and multimedia content. Users can enjoy an expansive virtual screen experience, bringing their favorite entertainment to life in a whole new way.

2. Music and Audio:

- The Spacetop G1's advanced audio capabilities enhance the music listening experience, whether users are streaming their favorite playlists or immersing themselves in virtual concerts and live performances. With spatial audio technology, users can enjoy rich, dynamic soundscapes that surround and envelop them.

3. Photography and Visual Arts:

- Creatives can leverage the Spacetop G1's AR-enhanced interface to explore photography, digital art, and visual storytelling in innovative ways. From editing photos in virtual darkrooms to collaborating on immersive art projects, the Spacetop G1 offers a versatile platform for creative expression.

Potential Uses in Gaming and Virtual Meetings

1. Gaming:

- The Spacetop G1 opens up exciting possibilities for gaming, with its immersive AR interface and powerful hardware capabilities. Gamers can dive into virtual worlds, interact with lifelike characters and environments, and experience gameplay like never before. Whether playing solo or participating in multiplayer experiences, the Spacetop G1 delivers an immersive and engaging gaming experience.

2. Virtual Meetings and Events:

- In the era of remote work and virtual collaboration, the Spacetop G1 redefines the concept of virtual meetings and events. Users can gather in virtual spaces, interact with colleagues and clients, and collaborate on projects in real time. With features such as spatial audio, virtual whiteboards, and interactive presentations, the Spacetop G1 facilitates seamless communication and collaboration across distances.

The Spacetop G1's multimedia capabilities and potential uses in gaming and virtual meetings demonstrate its versatility and adaptability across various domains. Whether users are seeking entertainment, creative expression, or professional collaboration, the Spacetop G1 offers a transformative platform that pushes the boundaries of spatial computing.

Troubleshooting the Spacetop G1: A Comprehensive Guide

Even with advanced technology like the Spacetop G1, users may encounter issues that require troubleshooting. Here's a detailed guide to help you address common problems and ensure your device operates smoothly.

1. Power and Battery Issues

- **Problem:** Device won't turn on or battery drains quickly.

- **Solution:** Ensure the Spacetop G1 is fully charged. Connect it to a power source using the provided USB-C charger. If the device still doesn't turn on, try a different power outlet or charger to rule out charger issues. For battery drain, close unnecessary applications, reduce screen brightness, and check for software updates that may include battery optimization fixes.

2. AR Glasses Connectivity

- **Problem:** AR glasses not connecting or displaying properly.

- Solution: Check the connection between the AR glasses and the laptop. Ensure the cable is securely plugged in. Restart both the Spacetop G1 and the AR glasses. If issues persist, inspect the cable for any damage and try using a different port.

3. Display Issues

- **Problem:** Poor image quality or no display in the AR glasses.

- **Solution:** Adjust the fit of the AR glasses for optimal viewing. Use the dimming button on the side of the glasses to enhance visibility in different lighting conditions. Ensure the AR glasses are clean and free of smudges. Update the SpaceOS to the latest version, as updates may contain display performance improvements.

4. Software and OS Issues

- **Problem:** SpaceOS is unresponsive or crashes frequently.

  - **Solution:** Restart the Spacetop G1. If the issue persists, perform a soft reset by holding down the power button for 10 seconds. Ensure all apps and the operating system are up-to-date. If problems continue, consider a factory reset (note that this will erase all data, so backup important files first).

5. Performance Issues

- **Problem:** Slow performance or lag.

  - **Solution:** Close unused applications and processes running in the background. Ensure the device has adequate free storage space; delete unnecessary files if needed. Check for and install any system updates. If performance issues persist, consider upgrading the storage or memory if possible.

6. Connectivity Issues

- **Problem:** Wi-Fi, Bluetooth, or 5G connectivity problems.

- **Solution:** Ensure the wireless settings are correctly configured and that the device is within range of the Wi-Fi router or Bluetooth device. Restart the router or modem. Forget the network and reconnect. For 5G issues, ensure you are in an area with 5G coverage and your plan supports 5G connectivity.

7. Audio Issues

- **Problem:** No sound or poor audio quality from the AR glasses.

- **Solution:** Check the volume settings and ensure they are not muted or too low. Inspect the AR glasses for any damage to the speakers. Restart the Spacetop G1 and the AR glasses. Update SpaceOS to the latest version, as updates may contain audio performance improvements.

8. Application Issues

- *Problem:* Apps not functioning properly or crashing.

- *Solution:* Update the apps to the latest versions. Clear the app cache and data from the settings menu. Uninstall and reinstall the problematic apps. If issues persist, contact the app developer for further assistance.

9. Hardware Issues

- *Problem:* Physical damage or malfunction.

- *Solution:* Inspect the Spacetop G1 and AR glasses for any visible damage. If you notice any physical issues, contact Sightful support for repair or replacement options. Do not attempt to open or repair the device yourself, as this may void the warranty.

General Troubleshooting Tips

- **Restart Regularly:** Regularly restart your device to keep it running smoothly.

- **Keep Software Updated:** Regularly check for and install software updates to ensure optimal performance and security.

- **Backup Data:** Regularly back up important data to prevent loss during troubleshooting or resets.

- **Consult User Manual:** Refer to the Spacetop G1 user manual for additional troubleshooting steps and tips.

By following these troubleshooting steps, you can resolve most common issues with the Spacetop G1 and ensure a smooth and productive user experience. For persistent problems, contacting Sightful's customer support for professional assistance is recommended.

www.ingramcontent.com/pod-product-compliance
Lightning Source LLC
Chambersburg PA
CBHW050238230526
45470CB00005B/2010